W9-BLK-885

Piano ★ Vocal ★ Guitar

Disney's

PRINCESS

Collection ★ Complete

Contents

ISBN 978-0-634-03387-2

Disney characters and artwork © Disney Enterprises, Inc.

Walt Disney Music Company
Wonderland Music Company, Inc.

DISTRIBUTED BY

HAL•LEONARD®
CORPORATION
7777 W. BLUEMOUND RD. P.O. BOX 13819 MILWAUKEE, WI 53213

The following songs are the property of:

BOURNE CO.
Music Publishers
5 West 37th Street
New York, NY 10018

I'm Wishing
One Song
Some Day My Prince Will Come
With A Smile And A Song

Visit Hal Leonard Online at
www.halleonard.com

BELLE

(Beauty and the Beast)
Lyrics by Howard Ashman
Music by Alan Menken

Little town, it's a quiet village.
Every day like the one before.
Little town full of little people
Waking up to say:

Bonjour! Bonjour!
Bonjour! Bonjour! Bonjour!

There goes the baker with his tray, like always,
The same old bread and rolls to sell.
Every morning just the same
Since the morning that we came
To this poor provincial town.

Look, there she goes, that girl is strange, no question.
Dazed and distracted, can't you tell?
Never part of any crowd,
'Cause her head's up on some cloud.
No denying she's a funny girl, that Belle.

Bonjour.
Good day.
How is your family?
Bonjour.
Good day.
How is your wife?
I need six eggs!
That's too expensive.
There must be more than this provincial life.

Look, there she goes, that girl is so peculiar.
I wonder if she's feeling well.
With a dreamy, far–off look
And her nose stuck in a book,
What a puzzle to the rest of us is Belle.

Oh, isn't this amazing?
It's my favorite part because…you'll see.
Here's where she meets Prince Charming,
But she won't discover that it's him 'til chapter three.

Now, it's no wonder that her name means "beauty."
Her looks have got no parallel.
But behind that fair facade,
I'm afraid she's rather odd.
Very different from the rest of us.
She's nothing like the rest of us.
Yes, different from the rest of us is Belle.

Right from the moment when I met her, saw her,
I said she's gorgeous and I fell.
Here in town there's only she
Who is beautiful as me,
So I'm making plans to woo and marry Belle.

Look, there he goes!
Isn't he dreamy?
Monsieur Gaston!
Oh, he's so cute!
Be still, my heart!
I'm hardly breathing!
He's such a tall, dark, strong and handsome brute.

Bonjour.
Pardon.
Good day.
Mais oui!
You call this bacon?
What lovely grapes!
Some cheese...
Ten yards.
One pound...
'Scuse me!
I'll get the knife.
Please let me through!
This bread...
Those fish...
It's stale!
They smell!
Madame's mistaken.

There must be more than this provincial life!
Just watch, I'm going to make Belle my wife!

Look, there she goes, a girl who's strange but special,
A most peculiar mademoiselle.
It's a pity and a sin.
She doesn't quite fit in
'Cause she really is a funny girl.
A beauty but a funny girl.
She really is a funny girl, that Belle!

BELLE
from Walt Disney's BEAUTY AND THE BEAST

Lyrics by HOWARD ASHMAN
Music by ALAN MENKEN

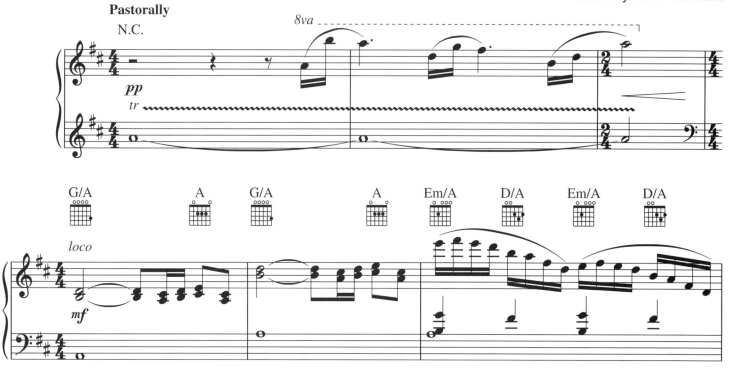

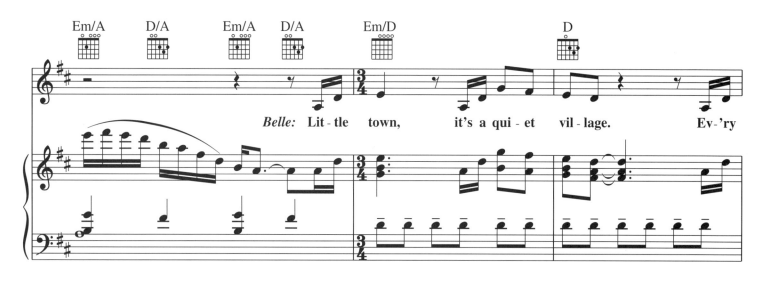

Belle: Lit-tle town, it's a qui-et vil-lage. Ev-'ry

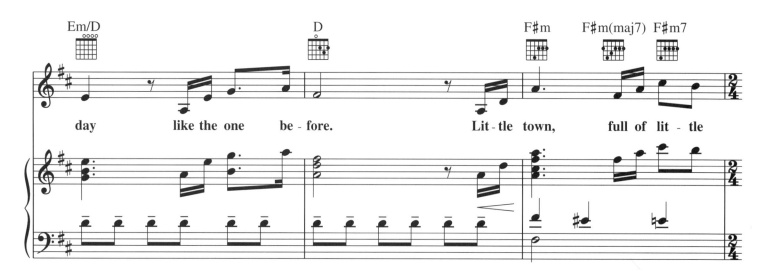

day like the one be-fore. Lit-tle town, full of lit-tle

rest of us. Yes, dif - f'rent from the rest of us is

Belle.

Pompously, a bit slower

CAN YOU FEEL THE LOVE TONIGHT

(The Lion King)
Music by Elton John
Lyrics by Tim Rice

Timon
I can see what's happening
(Pumbaa: What?)
And they don't have a clue.
(Pumbaa: Who?)
They'll fall in love and here's the bottom line:
Our trio's down to two.
(Pumbaa: Oh.)

The sweet caress of twilight;
There's magic everywhere.
And with all this romantic atmosphere,
Disaster's in the air.

Chorus
Can you feel the love tonight,
The peace the evening brings?
The world, for once, in perfect harmony
With all its living things.

Simba
So many things to tell her,
But how to make her see
The truth about my past? Impossible.
She'd turn away from me.

Nala
He's holding back, he's hiding.
But what I can't decide.
Why won't he be the king I know he is,
The king I see inside?

Chorus
Can you feel the love tonight,
The peace the evening brings?
The world, for once, in perfect harmony
With all its living things.

Can you feel the love tonight?
You needn't look too far.
Stealing through the night's uncertainties,
Love is where they are.

Timon
And if he falls in love tonight,
It can be assumed

Pumbaa
His carefree days with us are history,

Timon & Pumbaa
In short, our pal is doomed.

COLORS OF THE WIND

(Pocahontas)
Music by Alan Menken
Lyrics by Stephen Schwartz

You think I'm an ignorant savage
And you've been so many places
I guess it must be so
But still I cannot see
If the savage one is me
How can there be so much that you don't know?
You don't know...

You think you own whatever land you land on
The earth is just a dead thing you can claim
But I know ev'ry rock and tree and creature
Has a life, has a spirit, has a name

You think the only people who are people
Are the people who look and think like you
But if you walk the footsteps of a stranger
You'll learn things you never knew you never knew

Have you ever heard the wolf cry to the blue corn moon
Or asked the grinning bobcat why he grinned?
Can you sing with all the voices of the mountain?
Can you paint with all the colors of the wind?
Can you paint with all the colors of the wind?

Come run the hidden pine trails of the forest
Come taste the sun-sweet berries of the earth
Come roll in all the riches all around you
And for once, never wonder what they're worth

The rainstorm and the river are my brother
The heron and the otter are my friends
And we are all connected to each other
In a circle, in a hoop that never ends

How high does the sycamore grow?
If you cut it down, then you'll never know

And you'll never hear the wolf cry to the blue corn moon
For whether we are white or copper-skinned
We need to sing with all the voices of the mountain
Need to paint with all the colors of the wind
You can own the earth and still
All you'll own is earth until
You can paint with all the colors of the wind

Can You Feel The Love Tonight

from Walt Disney Pictures' THE LION KING

Music by ELTON JOHN
Lyrics by TIM RICE

COLORS OF THE WIND
from Walt Disney's POCAHONTAS

Music by ALAN MENKEN
Lyrics by STEPHEN SCHWARTZ

for - est, come taste the sun-sweet ber - ries of the earth; come

roll in all the rich - es all a - round you, and for once nev - er won - der what they're

worth. The rain - storm and the riv - er are my broth - ers; the

her - on and the ot - ter are my friends; and we are all con - nect - ed to each

A DREAM IS A WISH YOUR HEART MAKES

(Cinderella)
**Words and Music by Mack David,
Al Hoffman and Jerry Livingston**

A dream is a wish your heart makes
When you're fast asleep
In dreams you will lose your heartaches
Whatever you wish for, you keep
Have faith in your dreams and someday
Your rainbow will come smiling through
No matter how your heart is grieving
If you keep on believing
The dream that you wish will come true

...the dreams that I wish will come true

No matter how your heart is grieving
If you keep on believing
The dream that you wish will come true

HAIL TO THE PRINCESS AURORA

(Sleeping Beauty)
**Words by Tom Adair
Music by George Bruns**

Joyfully now to our princess we come,
Bringing gifts and all good wishes, too.
We pledge our loyalty anew.
Hail to the Princess Aurora!
All of her subjects adore her!
Hail to the King! Hail to the Queen!
Hail to the Princess Aurora!
Health to the princess!
Wealth to the princess!
Long live the Princess Aurora!
Hail Aurora!
Hail Aurora!
Health to the princess!
Wealth to the princess!
Long live the Princess Aurora!
Hail to the King! Hail to the Queen!
Hail to the Princess Aurora!

SLEEPING BEAUTY

(Sleeping Beauty)
**Words by Tom Adair
Music by George Bruns**

Sleeping Beauty fair,
Gold of sunshine in your hair,
Lips that shame the red, red rose,
Dreaming of true love in slumber repose.

One day he will come
Riding out of the dawn,
And you'll awaken to love's first kiss.
Till then, Sleeping Beauty, sleep on.

A DREAM IS A WISH YOUR HEART MAKES

from Walt Disney's CINDERELLA

Words and Music by MACK DAVID,
AL HOFFMAN and JERRY LIVINGSTON

HAIL TO THE PRINCESS AURORA/
SLEEPING BEAUTY

(Medley)

from Walt Disney's SLEEPING BEAUTY

Words by TOM ADAIR
Music by GEORGE BRUNS

Slightly slower, more freely

Ooh.

SLEEPING BEAUTY
Moderately slowly, expressively

Sleep - ing Beau - ty fair, gold of

sun - shine in your hair, lips that shame the

FORGET ABOUT LOVE

(The Return of Jafar)
**Words and Music by Michael Silversher
and Patty Silversher**

Iago
Forget about that guy.
Forget about the way you fell into his eyes.
Forget about his charms.
Forget about the way he held you in his arms.
Walking on air's obnoxious.
The thrills, the chills will make you nauseous
And you'll never get enough.
Just forget about love.

Forget about romance.
Forget about the way your heart begins to dance.
Then you feel the blush
When he's spouting out some sentimental mush.

Love really is revolting.
It's even worse than when you're molting.
Enough of this fluff.
Just forget about love.

Jasmine
I had almost forgotten the way it felt
When he held out his hand for mine.
My heart all a-flutter
(Iago: Oh, how I shudder!)
The first time we kissed.
(Iago: It won't be missed!)

Iago
Forget about his touch.
(Jasmine: I can't forget about his touch.)
In the scheme of things it doesn't matter much.
(Jasmine: It matters so much.)
You're better on your own.
A meal becomes a banquet when you eat alone.
(Jasmine: Mm.)

Jasmine & Iago
Love's filled with compromises.

Iago
And don't you hate those big surprises?

Jasmine
A cozy rendezvous.
(Iago: Oh, please!)
Candlelight for two.
(Iago: Oh, geez!)
Look, you're callin' my bluff.
I can't forget about love.

I can't forget about my heart
(Aladdin: I can't forget about my heart.)
And how it felt to fall for you right from the start.
(Aladdin: I'm still falling.)
Whatever we may do,
(Aladdin: Whatever we may do.)
You are here for me and I'll be there for you.
(Aladdin: I'll be there)

Both
To wish, to want, to wander,
To find the sun through rain and thunder.

Aladdin
A cozy rendezvous.
(Jasmine: Yes, please.)
Candlelight for two.
(Iago: Oh, geez!)

Iago
Enough is enough.

Jasmine & Aladdin
We can't forget about love.

FORGET ABOUT LOVE
from Walt Disney's THE RETURN OF JAFAR

Words and Music by MICHAEL SILVERSHER
and PATTY SILVERSHER

Iago: For - get a - bout__ that guy.

For - get a - bout__ the way you fell in - to his eyes.__ For -

get a - bout his charms.__ For - get a - bout__ the way he held you in his arms.__

Walk-ing on air's ob - nox - ious; the

thrills, the chills will make you nau - seous, and

you'll nev - er get e - nough. Just for - get a - bout love.

For - get a - bout ro - mance; for - get a - bout _ the way your

HOME
(Beauty and the Beast: The Broadway Musical)
Music by Alan Menken
Lyrics by Tim Rice

Yes, I made the choice
For Papa–I will stay
But I don't deserve to lose my freedom in this way
You monster!
If you think that what you've done is right, well then
You're a fool
Think again

Is this home?
Is this where I should learn to be happy?
Never dreamed
That a home could be dark and cold
I was taught
Every day in my childhood
Even when we grow old
Home will be where the heart is
Never were words so true
My heart's far, far away
Home is too

Is this home?
Is this what I must learn to believe in?
Try to find
Something good in this tragic place
Just in case
I should stay here forever
Held in this empty space
Oh, but that won't be easy
I know the reason why
My heart's far, far away
Home's a lie

What I'd give to return
To the life that I knew lately
But I know
That I can't
Solve my problems going back

Is this home?
Am I here for a day or forever?
Shut away
From the world until who knows when
Oh but then
As my life has been altered once
It can change again
Build higher walls around me
Change every lock and key

Nothing lasts
Nothing holds
All of me
My heart's far, far away
Home and free

I WON'T SAY (I'M IN LOVE)
(Hercules)
Music by Alan Menken
Lyrics by David Zippel

Meg
If there's a prize for rotten judgment,
I guess I've already won that.
No man is worth the aggravation.
That's ancient history, been there, done that.

Muses
Who d'ya think you're kiddin',
He's the Earth and heaven to you.
Try to keep it hidden,
Honey, we can see right through you.
Girl, ya can't conceal it,
We know how ya feel and who you're thinking of.

Meg
No chance, no way, I won't say it, no, no.

Muses
You swoon, you sigh, why deny it, uh oh.

Meg
It's too cliché, I won't say I'm in love.

I thought my heart had learned its lesson.
It feels so good when you start out.
My head is screaming, get a grip, girl,
Unless you're dying to cry your heart out.

Muses
You keep on denying
Who you are and how you're feeling.
Baby, we're not buying,
Hon, we saw ya hit the ceiling.
Face it like a grown–up,
When ya gonna own up that ya got, got, got it bad.

Meg
No chance, no way, I won't say it, no, no.

Muses
Give up, give in. Check the grin, you're in love.

Meg
This scene won't play, I won't say I'm in love.

Muses
You're doin' flips, read our lips: You're in love.

Meg
You're way off base, I won't say it.
Get off my case, I won't say it.

Muses
Girl, don't be proud, it's O.K. you're in love.

Meg
Oh.
At least out loud, I won't say I'm in love.

HOME

from Walt Disney's BEAUTY AND THE BEAST: THE BROADWAY MUSICAL

Music by ALAN MENKEN
Lyrics by TIM RICE

I WON'T SAY
(I'm in Love)
from Walt Disney Pictures' HERCULES

Music by ALAN MENKEN
Lyrics by DAVID ZIPPEL

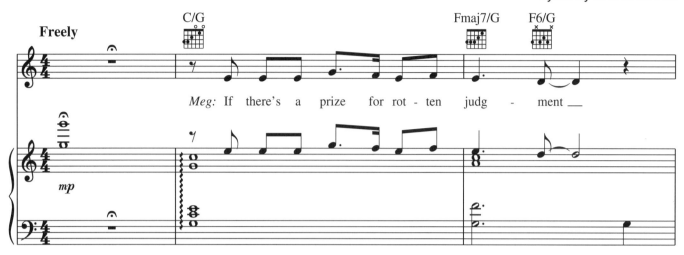

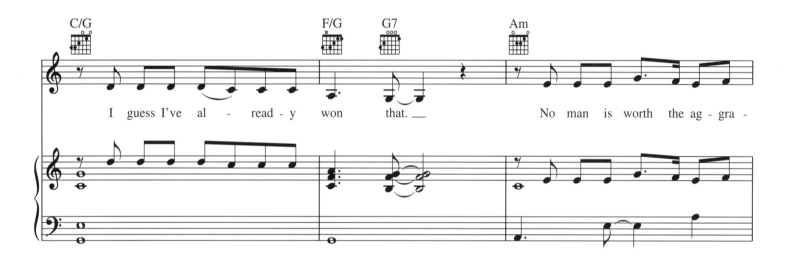

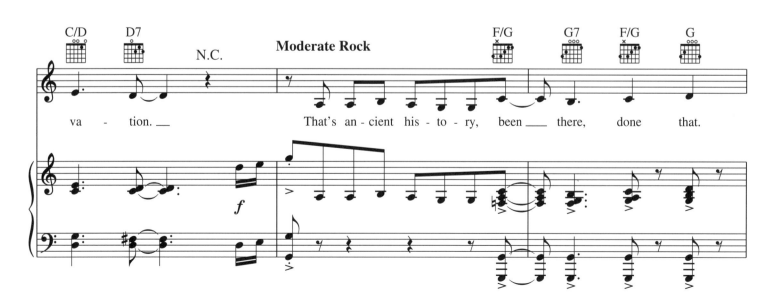

I WONDER
(Sleeping Beauty)
Words by Winston Hibler and Ted Sears
Music by George Bruns
Adapted from a Theme by Tchaikovsky

I wonder, I wonder
I wonder why each little bird has a someone
To sing to
Sweet things to
A gay little love melody?
I wonder, I wonder
If my heart keeps singing will my song go winging
To someone
Who'll find me
And bring back a love song to me?

KISS THE GIRL
(The Little Mermaid)
Lyrics by Howard Ashman
Music by Alan Menken

There you see her,
Sitting there across the way.
She don't got a lot to say,
But there's something about her.
And you don't know why,
But you're dying to try.
You wanna kiss the girl.

Yes, you want her.
Look at her, you know you do.
Possible she wants you, too.
There is one way to ask her.
It don't take a word,
Not a single word,
Go on and kiss the girl.

Sha la la la la la, my oh my,
Look like the boy too shy.
Ain't gonna kiss the girl.
Sha la la la la la, ain't that sad.
Ain't it a shame, too bad.
He gonna miss the girl.

Now's your moment,
Floating in a blue lagoon.
Boy, you better do it soon,
No time will be better.
She don't say a word
And she won't say a word
Until you kiss the girl.

Sha la la la la la, don't be scared.
You got the mood prepared,
Go on and kiss the girl.
Sha la la la la la, don't stop now.
Don't try to hide it how
You wanna kiss the girl.

Sha la la la la la, float along
And listen to the song,
The song say kiss the girl.
Sha la lila la la the music play.
Do what the music say.
You gotta kiss the girl.

You've got to kiss the girl.
You wanna kiss the girl.
You've gotta kiss the girl.
Go on and kiss the girl.

I'M WISHING/ONE SONG
(Snow White and the Seven Dwarfs)
Words by Larry Morey
Music by Frank Churchill

I'M WISHING
Wanna know a secret?
Promise not to tell?
We are standing by a wishing well
Make a wish into the well
That's all you have to do
And if you hear it echoing
Your wish will soon come true

I'm wishing (I'm wishing) for the one I love
To find me (to find me) today (today)
I'm hoping (I'm hoping), and I'm dreaming of
The nice things (the nice things) he'll say (he'll say)

I'm wishing (I'm wishing) for the one I love
To find me (to find me) today (today)

ONE SONG
Now that I've found you
Hear what I have to say
One song, I have but one song
One song, only for you
One heart tenderly beating
Ever entreating, constant and true

One love that has possessed me
One love, thrilling me through
One song, my heart keeps singing
Of one love
Only for you

IF I CAN'T LOVE HER
(Beauty and the Beast: The Broadway Musical)
Music by Alan Menken
Lyrics by Tim Rice

And in my twisted face
There's not the slightest trace
Of anything that even hints at kindness.
And from my tortured shape,
No comfort, no escape.
I see, but deep within is utter blindness.

Hopeless,
As my dream dies.
As the time flies,
Love a lost illusion.
Helpless,
Unforgiven.
Cold and driven
To this sad conclusion.

No beauty could move me,
No goodness improve me.
No power on Earth, if I can't love her.
No passion could reach me,
No lesson could teach me
How I could have loved her and make her love me too.
If I can't love her, then who?

Long ago, I should have seen
All the things I could have been.
Careless and unthinking, I moved onward!

No pain could be deeper.
No life could be cheaper.
No point anymore, if I can't love her.
No spirit could win me.
No hope left within me,
Hope I could have loved her and that she'd set me free.
But it's not to be.
If I can't love her,
Let the world be done with me.

I WONDER
from Walt Disney's SLEEPING BEAUTY

Words by WINSTON HIBLER and TED SEARS
Music by GEORGE BRUNS
Adapted from a Theme by TCHAIKOVSKY

KISS THE GIRL
from Walt Disney's THE LITTLE MERMAID

Lyrics by HOWARD ASHMAN
Music by ALAN MENKEN

Moderately

There you see her

sit-ting there a-cross the way. She don't got a lot to say,

but there's some-thing a-bout her. And you

I'M WISHING/ONE SONG
(Medley)
from Walt Disney's SNOW WHITE AND THE SEVEN DWARFS

Words by LARRY MOREY
Music by FRANK CHURCHILL

for the one I love to find me to - day. *Prince:* To - day.

ONE SONG

IF I CAN'T LOVE HER

from Walt Disney's BEAUTY AND THE BEAST: THE BROADWAY MUSICAL

Music by ALAN MENKEN
Lyrics by TIM RICE

Beast: And in my twist-ed face _____ there's not the slight-est trace _____ of an - y-thing that e - ven hints of kind - ness. And from my tor-tured shape, _____

JUST AROUND THE RIVERBEND

(Pocahontas)
Music by Alan Menken
Lyrics by Stephen Schwartz

What I love most about rivers is:
You can't step in the same river twice
The water's always changing, always flowing
But people, I guess, can't live like that
We all must pay a price
To be safe, we lose our chance of ever knowing
What's around the riverbend
Waiting just around the riverbend

I look once more
Just around the riverbend
Beyond the shore
Where the gulls fly free
Don't know what for
What I dream the day might send
Just around the riverbend
For me
Coming for me

I feel it there beyond those trees
Or right behind these waterfalls
Can I ignore that sound of distant drumming
For a handsome sturdy husband
Who builds handsome sturdy walls
And never dreams that something might be coming
Just around the riverbend?
Just around the riverbend

I look once more
Just around the riverbend
Beyond the shore
Somewhere past the sea
Don't know what for...
Why do all my dreams extend
Just around the riverbend?
Just around the riverbend...

Should I choose the smoothest course
Steady as the beating drum?
Should I marry Kocoum?
Is all my dreaming at an end?
Or do you still wait for me, Dream Giver
Just around the riverbend?

JUST AROUND THE RIVERBEND

from Walt Disney's POCAHONTAS

Music by ALAN MENKEN
Lyrics by STEPHEN SCHWARTZ

What I love most about rivers is: ___ you can't step in the same river twice. ___ The water's always changing, always flowing. ___ But people, I guess, can't live like that; ___ we

LOVE

(Robin Hood)
Words by Floyd Huddleston
Music by George Bruns

Love, it seems like only yesterday,
You were just a child at play.
Now you're all grown up inside of me.
Oh, how fast those moments flee.

Once we watched a lazy world go by.
Now the days seem to fly.
Life is brief, but when it's gone,
Love goes on and on.

Love will live, love will last.
Love goes on and on and on.

Once we watched a lazy world go by.
Now the days seem to fly.
Life is brief, but when it's gone,
Love goes on and on.

REFLECTION

(Mulan)
Music by Matthew Wilder
Lyrics by David Zippel

Look at me,
I will never pass for a perfect bride
Or a perfect daughter.
Can it be
I'm not meant to play this part?
Now I see
That if I were truly to be myself,
I would break my family's heart.

Who is that girl I see
Staring straight back at me?
Why is my reflection someone
I don't know?
Somehow I cannot hide
Who I am, though I've tried.
When will my reflection show
Who I am inside?
When will my reflection show
Who I am inside?

ONCE UPON A DREAM

(Sleeping Beauty)
Words and Music by Sammy Fain and Jack Lawrence
Adapted from a Theme by Tchaikovsky

I know you!
I walked with you once upon a dream
I know you!
The gleam in your eyes is so familiar a gleam
Yet I know it's true that visions are seldom all they seem
But if I know you
I know what you'll do
You'll love me at once
The way you did once upon a dream

But if I know you
I know what you'll do
You'll love me at once
The way you did once upon a dream

I know you!
I walked with you once upon a dream
I know you!
The gleam in your eyes is so familiar a gleam
And I know it's true that visions are seldom all they seem
But if I know you
I know what you'll do
You'll love me at once
The way you did once upon a dream

LOVE
from Walt Disney's ROBIN HOOD

Words by FLOYD HUDDLESTON
Music by GEORGE BRUNS

Love it seems like on-ly yes - ter -

day, You were just a child at

play. _____ Now you're

REFLECTION
from Walt Disney Pictures' MULAN

Music by MATTHEW WILDER
Lyrics by DAVID ZIPPEL

ONCE UPON A DREAM

from Walt Disney's SLEEPING BEAUTY

Words and Music by SAMMY FAIN
and JACK LAWRENCE
Adapted from a Theme by TCHAIKOVSKY

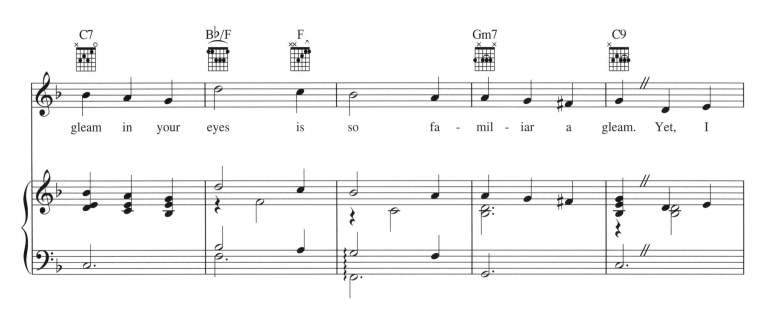

OUT OF THIN AIR

(Aladdin and the King of Thieves)
Words and Music by David Friedman

Jasmine
You showed me the world
When I was all locked up inside.
You reached out your hand
And took me on a magic carpet ride.

One look at your smile
And I could see the light
Shining everywhere.
People like you
Don't come out of thin air.

Aladdin
You don't understand.
There is so much that you don't see.
Just think if you can
What growing up had to be like for me.
Your father's a man
Who taught you who you are.
Mine was never there.
So how can you say
I don't come out of thin air?

There's so much I want to know.

Jasmine
You've got the chance to learn.

Aladdin
If it means I'd have to go...

Jasmine
I'll be right here when you return.

Our wedding can wait.
(Aladdin: I love you.)
I think it's worth this small delay.
(Aladdin: Maybe you're right.)
And won't it be great
To have your father see our wedding day?
(Aladdin: I've waited so long)
It isn't too late.
(Aladdin: To learn the truth.)

Both
And now at last
We can finally say

Jasmine
Your father is really there.

Aladdin
There's so much that we might share.

Jasmine
And you'll finally learn

Both
You don't come out of thin air.

PART OF YOUR WORLD

(The Little Mermaid)
Lyrics by Howard Ashman
Music by Alan Menken

Look at this stuff. Isn't it neat?
Wouldn't you think my collection's complete?
Wouldn't you think I'm the girl
The girl who has ev'rything?

Look at this trove, treasures untold
How many wonders can one cavern hold?
Looking around here, you'd think
Sure, she's got ev'rything

I've got gadgets and gizmos a-plenty
I've got who-zits and what-zits galore
You want thing-a-ma-bobs? I've got twenty
But who cares? No big deal. I want more

I wanna be where the people are
I wanna see, wanna see 'em dancin'
Walkin' around on those
Whaddya call 'em? Oh, feet

Flippin' your fins, you don't get too far
Legs are required for jumpin', dancin'
Strollin' along down the
What's that word again? Street

Up where they walk, up where they run
Up where they stay all day in the sun
Wanderin' free, wish I could be
Part of that world

What would I give if I could live
Outta these waters?
What would I pay to spend a day
Warm on the sand?

Betcha on land they understand
Bet they don't reprimand their daughters
Bright young women, sick of swimmin'
Ready to stand

And ready to know what the people know
Ask 'em my questions and get some answers
What's a fire?–and why does it
What's the word? Burn

When's it my turn?
Wouldn't I love, love to explore
That shore up above, out of the sea
Wish I could be part of that world

OUT OF THIN AIR
from Walt Disney's ALADDIN AND THE KING OF THIEVES

Words and Music by
DAVID FRIEDMAN

PART OF YOUR WORLD
from Walt Disney's THE LITTLE MERMAID

Lyrics by HOWARD ASHMAN
Music by ALAN MENKEN

Moderately bright

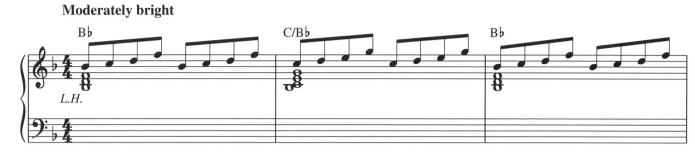

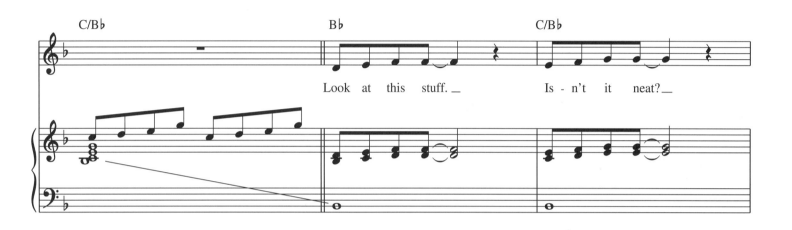

Look at this stuff. __ Is - n't it neat? __

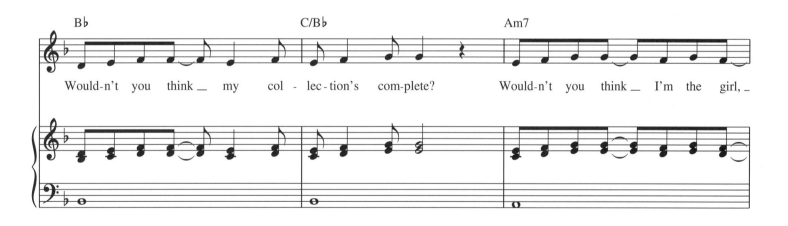

Would-n't you think __ my col - lec - tion's com-plete? Would-n't you think __ I'm the girl, __

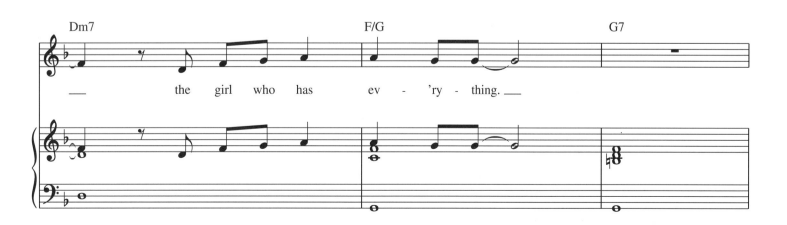

__ the girl who has ev - 'ry - thing. __

Look at this trove, _ treas - ures un - told. _ How man - y won - ders can

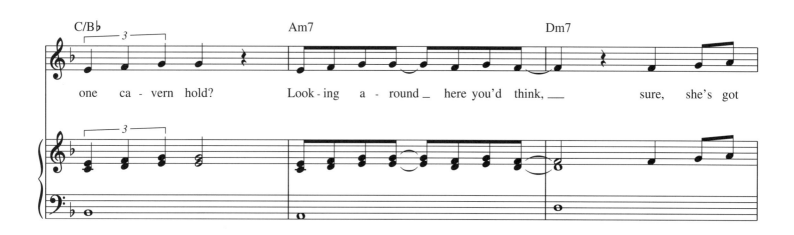

one ca - vern hold? Look - ing a - round _ here you'd think, __ sure, she's got

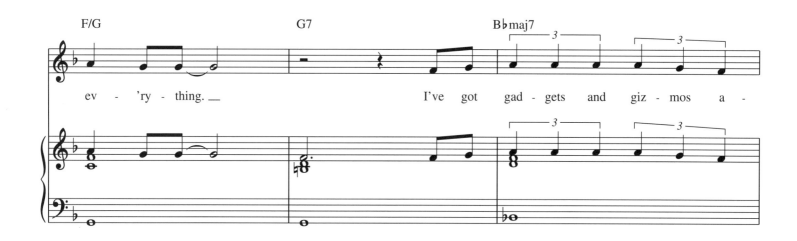

ev - 'ry - thing. _ I've got gad - gets and giz - mos a -

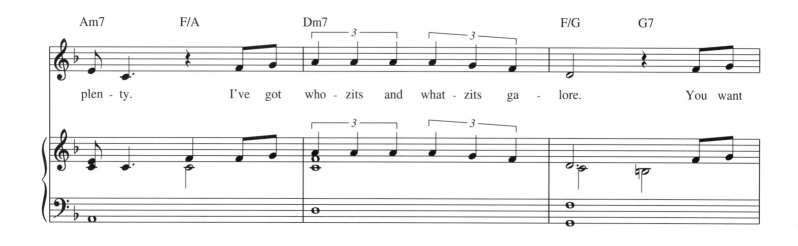

plen - ty. I've got who - zits and what - zits ga - lore. You want

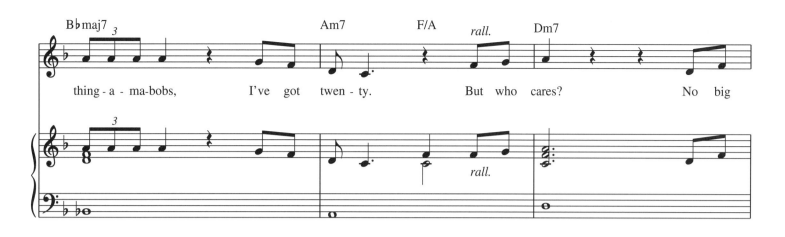

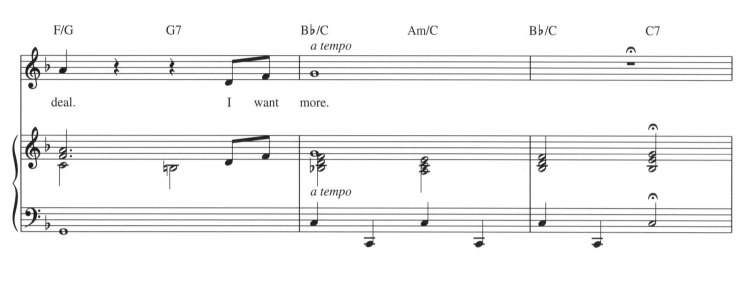

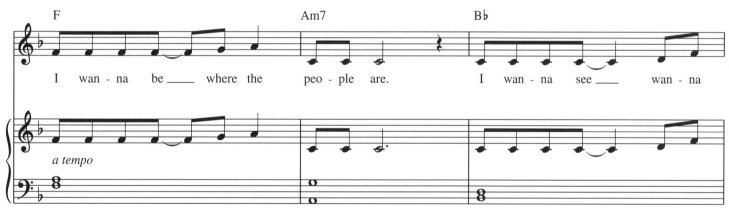

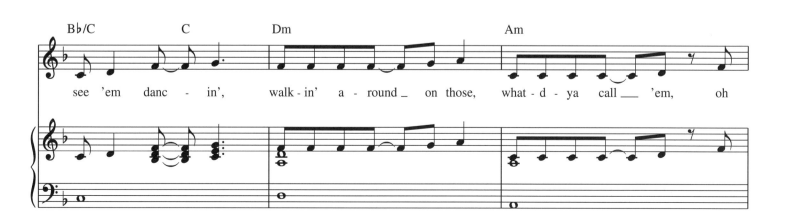

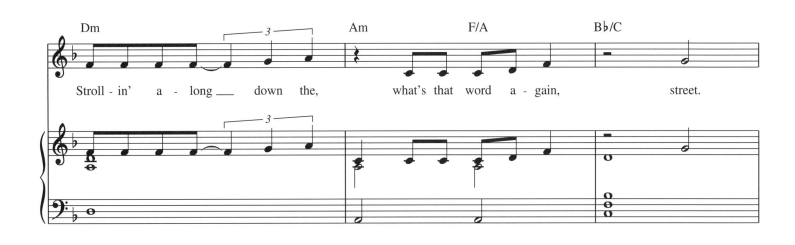

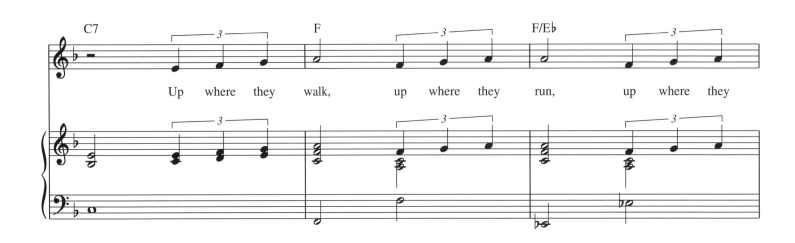

slower

F

out of the sea.

Wish I could

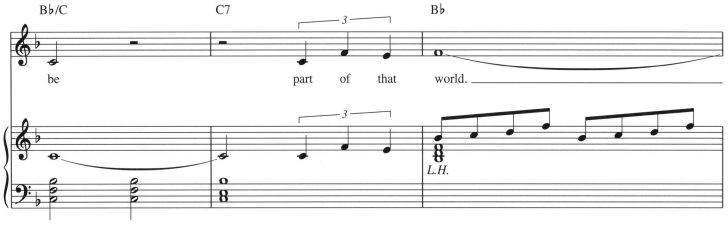

slower

Bb/C   C7   Bb

be   part of that world.

L.H.

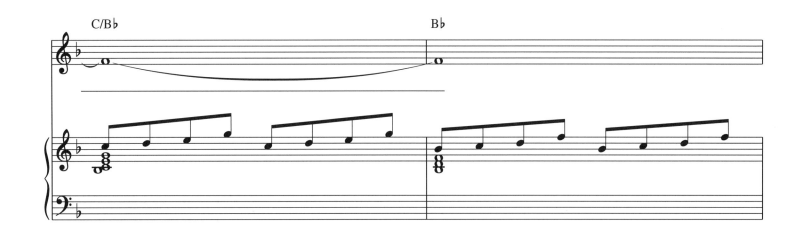

C/Bb   Bb

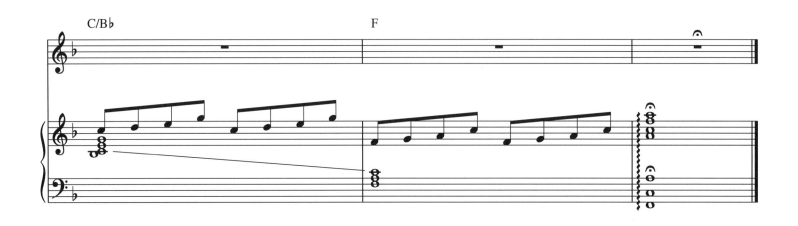

C/Bb   F

SO THIS IS LOVE

(Cinderella)
**Words and Music by Mack David,
Al Hoffman and Jerry Livingston**

Mmm, mmm
So this is love, mmm
So this is love
So this is what makes life divine
I'm all aglow, mmm
And now I know (And now I know)
The key to all heaven is mine

My heart has wings, mmm
And I can fly
I'll touch ev'ry star in the sky
So this is the miracle that I've been dreaming of
Mmm, mmm, so this is love

SOME DAY MY PRINCE WILL COME

(Snow White and the Seven Dwarfs)
**Words by Larry Morey
Music by Frank Churchill**

Someday my prince will come
Someday we'll meet again
And away to his castle we'll go
To be happy forever I know

Someday when spring is here
We'll find our love anew
And the birds will sing
And wedding bells will ring
Someday when my dreams come true

SO THIS IS LOVE
(The Cinderella Waltz)
from Walt Disney's CINDERELLA

Words and Music by MACK DAVID,
AL HOFFMAN and JERRY LIVINGSTON

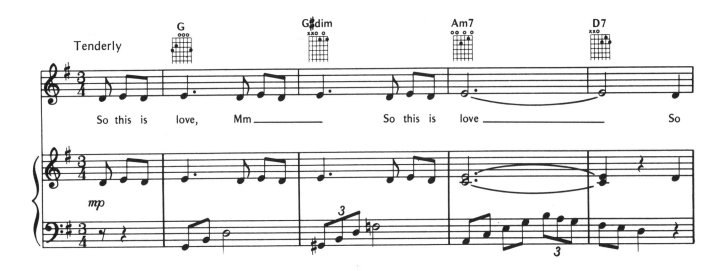

So this is love, Mm _____ So this is love _____ So

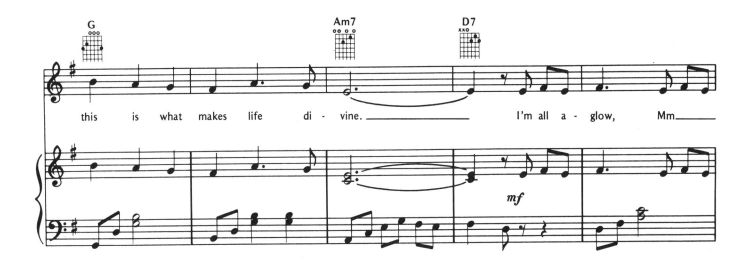

this is what makes life di - vine. _____ I'm all a - glow, Mm_____

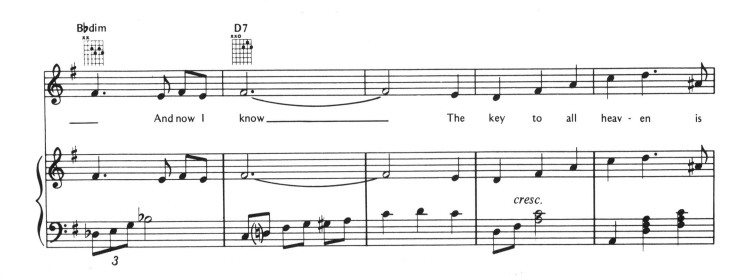

_____ And now I know _____ The key to all heav - en is

SOME DAY MY PRINCE WILL COME

from Walt Disney's SNOW WHITE AND THE SEVEN DWARFS

Words by LARRY MOREY
Music by FRANK CHURCHILL

SOMETHING THERE

(Beauty and the Beast)
Lyrics by Howard Ashman
Music by Alan Menken

Belle
There's something sweet
And almost kind
But he was mean, and he was coarse and unrefined
And now he's dear and so unsure
I wonder why I didn't see it there before?

Beast
She glanced this way, I thought I saw
And when we touched she didn't shudder at my paw
No, it can't be...I'll just ignore
But then she's never looked at me that way before

Belle
New and a bit alarming
Who'd have ever thought that this could be?
True that he's no Prince Charming
But there's something in him
That I simply didn't see

Lumiere
Well, who'd have thought

Mrs. Potts
Well, bless my soul

Cogsworth
Well, who'd have known

Mrs. Potts
Well, who indeed?

Lumiere
And who'd have guessed they'd come
Together on their own?

Mrs. Potts
It's so peculiar

Mrs. Potts/Lumiere/Cogsworth
Well, wait and see, a few days more
There may be something there that
Wasn't there before

Cogsworth
You know, perhaps there is something there that
Wasn't there before

Mrs. Potts
There may be something there that
Wasn't there before

THERE'S ONLY ONE ARIEL

(Songs from the Sea)
Words and Music by Janis Liebhart and Alan O'Day

We play games like other girls.
We love to dress up in shells and pearls.
But she's off in her own little world.
There's only one Ariel.

She's got the prettiest voice in the sea,
But she's never here when she ought to be.
She's the missing note in our harmony.
You're late again, Ariel.

La la la. She's a dreamer.
There's a faraway look in her eyes.
La la la. Have you seen her
Swimming far too high
Where the ocean meets the sky?

She brings stuff home from everywhere.
Her room's a mess; she doesn't care.
There's hardly room for her in there.
Clean it up, Ariel.

La la la. She's a dreamer.
There's a faraway look in her eyes.
La la la. Have you seen her
Swimming far too high
Where the ocean meets the sky?

So if you're swimming in the sea one day
And a pretty little mermaid wants to play,
We bet you'll know her right away.
There's only one Ariel.

Ariel.
There's only one Ariel.
Ariel.

SOMETHING THERE

from Walt Disney's BEAUTY AND THE BEAST

Lyrics by HOWARD ASHMAN
Music by ALAN MENKEN

THERE'S ONLY ONE ARIEL

from SONGS FROM THE SEA

Words and Music by JANIS LIEBHART
and ALAN O'DAY

Ariel's Sister I (spoken): Has anyone seen Ariel?   She hasn't picked out the sea pearls she's

going to wear tonight.   Sister II: We daughters of Triton must look our best at the mermaids' ball.

Sisters: Why can't she be like the rest of us?   Sisters (sung):   We play games like

WITH A SMILE AND A SONG

(Snow White and the Seven Dwarfs)
Words by Larry Morey
Music by Frank Churchill

With a smile and a song,
Life is just like a bright sunny day;
Your cares fade away,
And your heart is young.

With a smile and a song,
All the world seems to waken anew,
Rejoicing with you,
As the song is sung.

There's no use in grumbling,
When raindrops come tumbling;
Remember you're the one
Who can fill the world with sunshine.

When you smile and you sing,
Everything is in tune and it's Spring
And Life flows along,
With a smile and a song.

A WHOLE NEW WORLD

(Aladdin)
Music by Alan Menken
Lyrics by Tim Rice

Aladdin
I can show you the world
Shining, shimmering, splendid
Tell me, princess, now when did
You last let your heart decide?

I can open your eyes
Take you wonder by wonder
Over, sideways, and under
On a magic carpet ride

A whole new world
A new fantastic point of view
No one to tell us no
Or where to go
Or say we're only dreaming

Jasmine
A whole new world
A dazzling place I never knew
But when I'm way up here
It's crystal clear
That now I'm in a whole new world
With you

Aladdin
Now I'm in a whole new world with you

Jasmine
Unbelievable sights
Indescribable feeling
Soaring, tumbling, freewheeling
Through an endless diamond sky
A whole new world
(Aladdin: Don't you dare close your eyes)
A hundred thousand things to see
(Aladdin: Hold your breath–it gets better)

Jasmine
I'm like a shooting star
I've come so far
I can't go back to where I used to be

Aladdin
A whole new world
(Jasmine: Every turn a surprise)
With new horizons to pursue
(Jasmine: Every moment, red letter)

Both
I'll chase them anywhere
There's time to spare
Let me share this whole new world with you

Aladdin
A whole new world
(Jasmine: A whole new world)
That's where we'll be
(Jasmine: That's where we'll be)

Aladdin
A thrilling chase

Jasmine
A wondrous place

Both
For you and me

WITH A SMILE AND A SONG
from Walt Disney's SNOW WHITE AND THE SEVEN DWARFS

Words by LARRY MOREY
Music by FRANK CHURCHILL

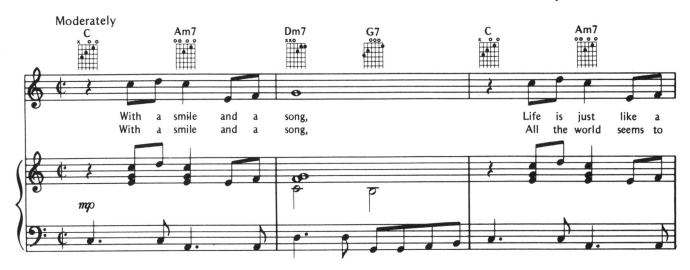

With a smile and a song,
With a smile and a song,

Life is just like a
All the world seems to

bright sun-ny day, Your cares fade a-way,____ And your heart is
wak-en a-new, Re-joic-ing with you,____ As the song is

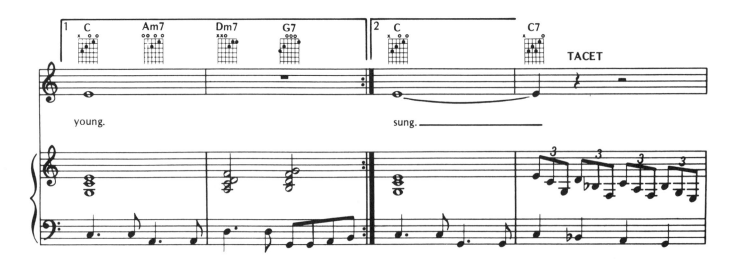

young.
sung.

TACET

A WHOLE NEW WORLD

from Walt Disney's ALADDIN

Music by ALAN MENKEN
Lyrics by TIM RICE